In the Box

words by Joelie Croser
photographs by Francesco Bozzo

What can I feel?

This feels small.

This feels big.

This feels long.

This feels short.

This feels hard.

This feels soft.

This feels thick.

This feels thin.

This feels bumpy.

This feels smooth.

This feels flat.

14

This feels round.

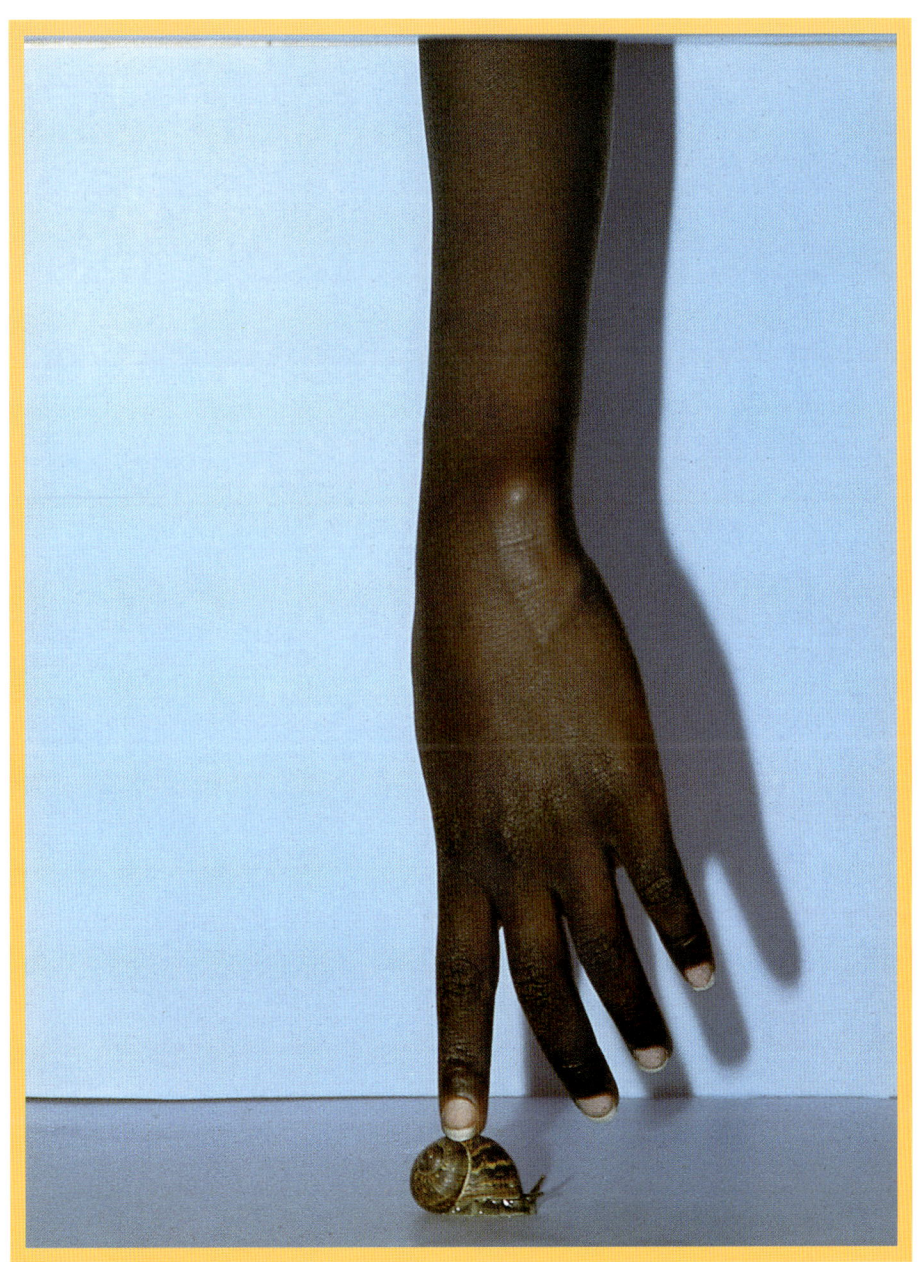

This feels slimy.